Welcome to Your Adventure!

This workbook is your special jour
carefully about each part, and ren
experiences really matter. Embrace who you are, because g
you a unique view of the world!

What is a Therian?

Being a Therian isn't a religion or a lifestyle choice it's something deep inside, just like how someone knows their gender. The word "Therian" comes from the Greek word "therion", which means "beast" or "wild animal".

A Therian is someone who feels like they have the spirit or mind of an animal, even though they look human on the outside. They feel a strong identity with a specific animal, like a wolf, a bird, or a cat, and might think or act in ways that remind them of that animal. It's like having an animal as a part of who they are!

What is Therianthropy?

Therianthropy is all about feeling connected to a non-human animal in a special way. It's more than just liking animals it's feeling like you share a part of your spirit or personality with one, even though you're still human on the outside. Therians can be very different from each other, because we all identify with different species (our theriotypes).

A Bit of History

The idea of people feeling connected to animals has been around for centuries! In ancient stories, there were tales of people who could change into animals or had animal spirits. Think about werewolves from old European stories or Native American shamans who believed they could become animals. These are early examples of how people have always felt a special link with animals.

Ready to explore more? Let's begin!

UNDERSTANDING THERIANS: A FUN GUIDE TO THERIANTHROPY

Therianthropy vs. Furry Fandom
Sometimes people mix up Therians and Furries, but they're actually different! Furries are fans who love creating or enjoying stories, art, and role-playing with animal characters that have human traits (like talking or walking on two legs). Therians, on the other hand, feel a deep, personal identity to real animals either in their mind or spirit.

Do Therians Think They Can Turn into Animals?
Nope! Therians don't believe they can physically turn into animals. Instead, they feel like they have the mindset of their animal, called their "Theriotype". Some might imagine having animal features like ears or a tail during an experience known as "shifting", but they know these changes aren't real and they're just strong feelings or mental shifts.

Is Therianthropy a Mental Illness?
No, Therianthropy isn't a mental illness. It's simply a part of a person's identity, like how people identify with their culture or beliefs. Most Therians live happy, healthy lives, and their connection to their Theriotype is a natural part of who they are. It's important to understand the difference between mental health and personal identity.

Do All Therians Feel the Same?
Not at all! Every Therian's experience is different. Some might feel connected to just one animal, while others feel close to several. The way they experience their connection can also vary. Some feel it strongly, while others might feel it only sometimes. It's a very personal thing!

THIS THERIAN WORKBOOK IS DEDICATED TO YOU.
YOU'VE GOT THIS.

THIS BOOK BELONGS TO:

Therians must always act like their animal
Some people believe that Therians constantly behave like their Theriotype (the animal they identify with), but this isn't true. While a Therian might sometimes feel or act in ways that reflect their connection to their animal, they don't always act like that. Therians still live everyday human lives like going to school, work and interacting with others. Their connection to their Theriotype is often more internal and personal rather than something that influences their behavior all the time.

Therians can communicate with animals
A common misconception is that Therians believe they can talk too or understand animals in a supernatural way. While Therians often feel a strong connection to their Theriotype, they don't claim to have special powers that let them communicate directly with animals. Their bond with animals is more about personal identity and inner feelings, not magical abilities.

Therians only identity with wild animals
Many people think Therians only identify with wild animals like wolves, tigers, or eagles, but that's not always true. Therians can feel connected to any kind of animal, including mythical creatures like dragons, mermaids or unicorns The important part is the deep connection they feel, whether it's with a wild animal, mythical or one you'd find at home!

Understanding Therianthropy
Therianthropy is all about recognising that people have unique and different identities. For Therians, their connection to animals is a special part of who they are, adding to the rich diversity of human experience and expression.

So, it's important to stay open-minded and appreciate the different ways people see and understand themselves!

Being yourself is your greatest superpower!

TYPES OF THERIANTHROPY

Therians

Who are they? Therians feel a deep connection to one or more specific animals, believing that part of their identity or spirit is like that animal.

Example: A person might feel connected to a wolf, experiencing moments where they think or sense the world in a wolf-like way.

Cladotherians

Who are they? Cladotherians feel connected to a whole group or family of animals, not just one specific species.

Example: Instead of feeling connected to just lions, a Cladotherian might feel linked to all big cats, like lions, tigers, and leopards.

Polytherians

Who are they? Polytherians feel connected to more than one specific animal, but at different times.

Example: Someone might feel like a wolf one day and a raven on another day, switching between animals depending on their feelings.

Contherians

Who are they? Contherians always feel like their animal without any shifts or changes. It's a constant part of who they are.

Example: If someone feels like a fox, they always feel like a fox in their daily life, no matter what they're doing.

Suntherians

Who are they? Suntherians feel their connection to their animal at all times, but it can be stronger or weaker depending on the situation. Unlike shifts, which are big changes, their connection stays there, just with different intensity.

Example: A person might always feel like a cat, but sometimes they feel more cat-like when they're relaxed or playful, and other times the feeling is less intense.

SHIFTS

A "shift" is when a Therian starts feeling or acting more like the animal they connect with. It's like if you're playing a game where you pretend to be a cat, and suddenly you really start feeling like you are a cat thinking about how a cat thinks or feeling what a cat might feel. It doesn't mean they turn into an animal, but inside, they feel a lot like that animal for a while.

It's important to note that not every Therian experiences shifts, and that's okay. Some Therians feel a constant connection to their animal side and don't shift at all. If you do shift, though, it's important to know that it can look and feel very different for everyone.

Types of Shifts

Mental Shifts (M-Shifts)

What happens? Therians think and act like their animal.
Example: They might see, hear, or react like their animal, such as having sharper senses or different behaviours.

Phantom Shifts (P-Shifts)

What happens? Therians feel like they have parts of their animal that aren't really there.
Example: They might feel like they have a tail, wings, or fur, even though they don't. This feeling is very real to them.

Dream Shifts

What happens? Dream shifts (D-Shifts) happen when a Therian dreams about being their animal.
Details: These dreams can feel very real and show the animal's behaviours, environments, and experiences.
Why it matters: Dream shifts can help Therians understand their animal identity better and make them feel more connected to it.

QUIZ

Answer the questions below to see which animal matches your inner spirit. Remember, this is just for fun it doesn't mean anything, but who knows? You might discover something new about yourself along the way!

Quiz Questions

When you are in nature, which place do you feel most at home in?
a) Forest
b) Mountains
c) Desert
d) Sea or ponds
e) Fields or grasslands

Which activity do you enjoy the most?
a) Running or walking
b) Climbing or exploring heights
c) Sunbathing or relaxing in warm places
d) Swimming or being near water
e) Observing or moving stealthily

When you dream, which animals do you see or feel connected to?
a) Wolf or dog
b) Bird or eagle
c) Snake or lizard
d) Fish or dolphin
e) Big cat or deer

QUIZ

How do you react to stress or danger?
a) Face it head-on and protect others
b) Find a high place or retreat to a safe spot
c) Stay still and watch before acting
d) Swim away or move smoothly through it
e) Blend in or move quietly

Which best describes your social behaviour?
a) Loyal and protective in a group
b) Independent but likes socialising
c) Prefers to be alone or in small groups
d) Social and playful in a group
e) Observant and strategic with others

What type of food do you prefer?
a) Meat-based diet
b) Mixed diet with lots nuts and seeds
c) Both meat and vegetables/fruit
d) Seafood or vegetable-based diet
e) Fresh and natural foods

Which best describes your personality?
a) Brave and protective
b) Free-spirited and adventurous
c) Patient and observant
d) Adaptable and intuitive
e) Graceful and strategic

Therianthropy can be experienced in many different ways, making every Therian's journey unique!

Quiz Results
Count how many times you picked each letter (a, b, c, d, e) to
see which one you chose the most.

Mostly a's:
Your Theriotype might be a land predator like a wolf or big dog.
You are protective and loyal and value your community.

Mostly b's:
Your Theriotype could be a bird of prey or a mountain animal.
You are adventurous, enjoy heights, and like being independent.

Mostly c's:
Your Theriotype might be a reptile or desert animal. You are
observant and patient, and you like warm, sunny places.

Mostly d's:
Your Theriotype could be an aquatic animal like a fish or
dolphin. You are adaptable and intuitive, and you love being
near water.

Mostly e's:
Your Theriotype might be a stealthy or graceful animal like a big
cat or deer. You are strategic, observant, and value your privacy.

How long have you identified with your Therian form?

What animal do you feel most connected to, and what traits or behaviours of that animal do you see in yourself?

Describe the moment you realised you were a Therian.
What emotions and thoughts did you experience?

I am enough, just the way I am.

ANIMAL IDENTITY

How do you feel when you embrace your connection to your animal identity? Do you feel stronger and more confident, or calm and in tune with nature?

NATURE INTERACTION

Describe a recent experience in nature.
How did it make you feel as a Therian?

SHIFT EXPERIENCES

Describe any recent shifts you've had. Were they mental, phantom, or dream shifts? How did you feel during and after the shift?

CHALLENGES

What challenges do you face as a Therian?
How do you cope with them?

In a world full of humans, it's okay to feel a connection to something more. Let your true self shine.

THERIAN COMMUNITY

Do you have a supportive community or friends
around you and who are they?

THERIAN COMMUNITY

Write about your involvement in the Therian community.
How has connecting with other Therians impacted your journey?

What kinds of activities or games do you like to do that make you feel more like the animal you feel connected to?

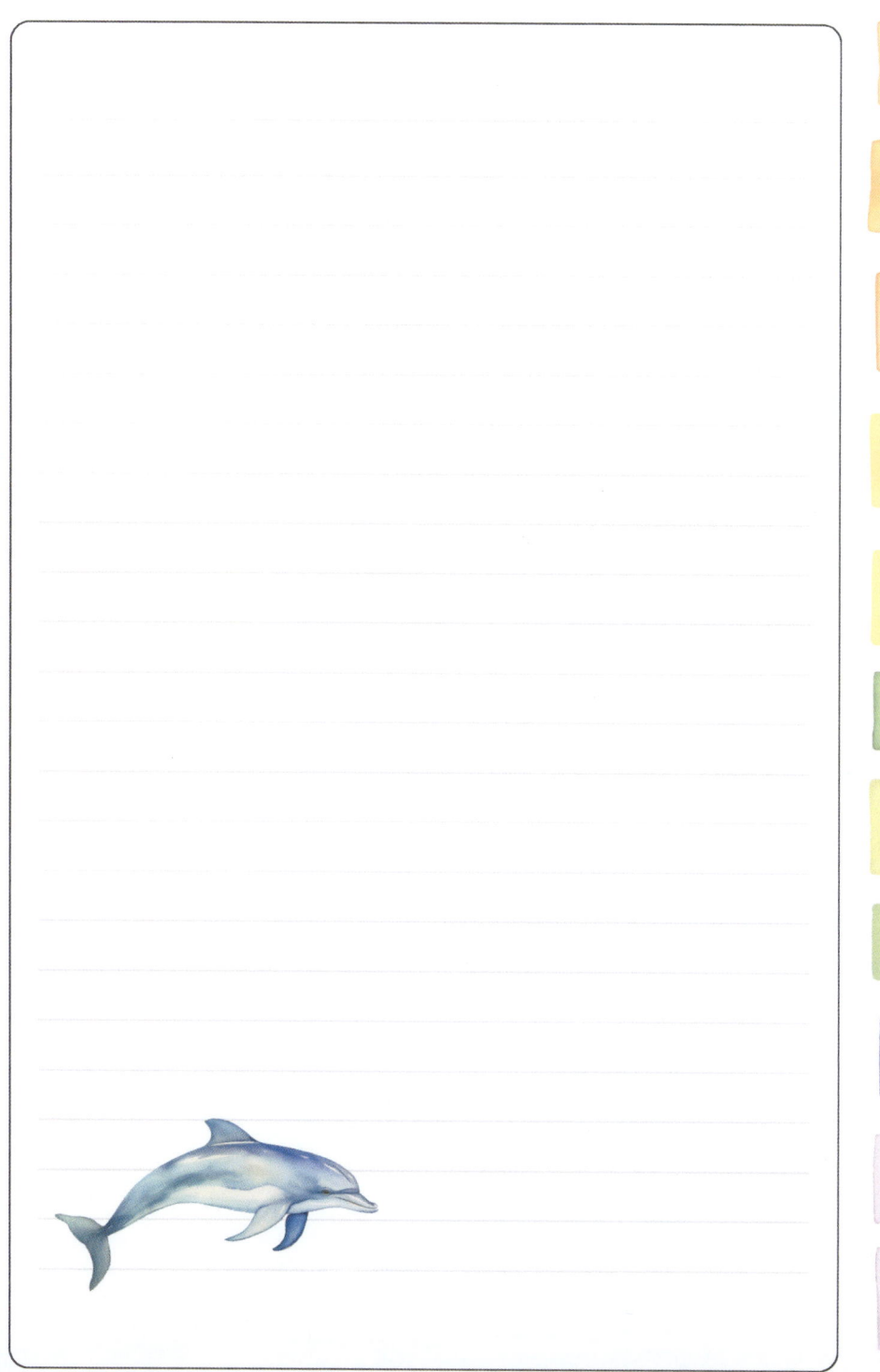

YOUR ENVIRONMENT

What places or things make you feel happiest when your connected with your animal side?

SELF-DISCOVERY

How has your journey as a Therian helped you discover more about yourself? What have you learned?

What are your Therian's strengths and weaknesses?

What are your likes and dislikes

I deserve to be happy and loved just as I am.

Does your Therian form give you a unique ability or particular trait?

Do you have any Therian gear? If you do, what is it? If not, what kind of gear would you like to have?

What foods or snacks do you enjoy that feel connected to your Therian identity?

Do you experience any specific sensitivities or dislikes in your Therian form?

Are there any parts of your Therian journey that make you feel nervous or worried?

Your animal side is a strength, not a weakness. It's what makes you unique.

How do you mix your animal feelings with your everyday human life?
Do they fit together well, or are there times when they clash?

As a Therian, how do you respond to conflicts or encounters with other species? This can show your feelings, values, and beliefs.

Embrace your inner animal. it's a wild and wonderful part of who you are.

What are your hopes and aspirations as a Therian?
How do you see your journey evolving in the future?

What are your goals or dreams?

What strategies do you use to manage any negative emotions or experiences related to being a Therian?

Does being a Therian connect with your spiritual beliefs in any way? If so, how?

The world needs more people who understand and respect nature.

As a Therian, you're a bridge between the two.

How does society's perception of Therians affect you?
How do you navigate these perceptions?

Describe any creative activities (like art, music or writing) that help you express your Therian identity.

CREATIVE EXPRESSION

Create A Piece Of Art Representing Your Therian Style

Let's do a fun art activity to explore your inner animal! Think about an animal you feel connected to. It could be any animal you love or feel a special bond with. Now, let's create some art to show that connection.

Draw Your Animal: Use coloured pencils, markers, or paint to draw a picture of your animal. Imagine yourself as that animal and add details that show its personality and environment.

Reflect On Your Creation
- Once you've completed your artwork, take a moment to reflect on it.

- What parts of your Therian identity show up in your art?

- How did creating this piece make you feel?

CREATIVE EXPRESSION

Create A Mask Representing Your Therian Style

Animal Mask

Make a mask of your animal identity. Use cardboard or paper plates, and decorate it with paints, markers and other craft supplies.

Wear the mask and try acting like the animal how does it move? What sounds does it make?

This activity is all about letting your imagination run wild and having a blast while expressing who you truly are!

CREATIVE EXPRESSION

Write a story

Story Time

Write a short story about an adventure you go on as your chosen animal. What special skills or instincts do you have? Who do you meet? What challenges do you face?

Keep in mind, this story-writing activity is all about letting your creativity shine and having fun with your imagination!

Design Your Therian's Habitat Or Create A Den

Imagine the perfect place for your Theriotype to live.

Draw a detailed picture of your animal's home what kind of environment do they feel most comfortable in? Is it a forest, desert, or maybe a snowy mountain?

Add details like plants, other animals and anything else that would make your Theriotype happy!

Bonus: Write a short description of what a day in this habitat would be like for your animal side.

I am connected to the earth, the sky, and the animals around me.

Create A Piece Of Art Representing Your Therian Style

Let's make something awesome! This exercise is all about designing a flag that shows off your unique Therian side. Your flag is like a super cool badge that represents who you are.

Think About Your Animal Side

What animal do you identify most with? What colours or patterns do you think of when you picture them?
What awesome traits do you share with this animal? Maybe you're strong, sneaky or super fast!

Consider the traits and values that define your Therian.

Choose Your Colours and Symbols

Choose colours that totally scream YOU!
Add symbols or patterns that remind you of your animal side something that makes your flag look super cool and meaningful.

Design Your Flag

Use the next few pages to start sketching! Don't worry about being perfect just have fun with it.
Think about how the colours and symbols tell the story of your Therian self.

Extra Fun. Share Your Flag!

If you want, show off your flag to friends or the Therian community. Your design might inspire someone else!

Remember, this activity is all about letting your creativity flow and enjoying the fun of using your imagination!

Animal Senses Scavenger Hunt
Take a walk outside and imagine you're using your Theriotype's senses.

Make a list of things to find that your animal might notice, like a certain smell, sound or sight.

For example, if your Theriotype is a wolf, try to notice sounds from far away or the scent of plants and flowers.
Bonus: After the walk, write down how it felt to use your animal senses.

Animal Movement Challenge
Pick a space indoors or outdoors where you can move around safely and try moving like your Theriotype!

If you identify with a bird, try flapping your arms and imagine flying.
If you're a big cat, practice silent, sneaky steps like you're stalking prey.

Think about how your animal moves and see how well you can mimic it.

Bonus: Challenge a friend or family member to guess your Theriotype based on your movements!

Therian Dream Journal
Keep a dream journal to track any dreams where you connect with your Theriotype.

After waking up, write down any details of the dream. Did you feel like your animal self? What did you see, feel or experience?
Over time, look back at your journal to see if you notice any patterns or messages from your animal identity.

Bonus: Draw a picture of one of your most powerful dreams, showing how your Theriotype was involved.

COVER THESE PAGES WITH POSITIVE WORDS ABOUT YOU

GRAB YOUR FAVOURITE PEN OR MARKERS AND FILL THESE PAGES WITH ALL THE POSITIVE WORDS AND PHRASES THAT DESCRIBE HOW BRILLIANT YOU ARE.

THINK ABOUT:

- THE COOL THINGS THAT MAKE YOU, YOU!. ARE YOU KIND, BRAVE OR CREATIVE?

- WHAT DO YOU LOVE ABOUT YOUR THERIAN SIDE.

- WHAT ACHIEVEMENTS ARE YOU PROUD OF, BIG OR SMALL.

THERE ARE NO RULES JUST FILL THIS PAGE WITH EVERYTHING THAT MAKES YOU SHINE.

REMEMBER, YOU'RE ONE-OF-A-KIND AND TOTALLY AWESOME!

My bond with my animal self makes me strong and brave.

Write about any important dreams that felt connected to your Therian side. What did you learn or take away from them?

PERSONAL SYMBOLS

Are there any symbols, objects, or rituals that hold special meaning for you as a Therian? Explain their significance.

Who in your life supports your Therian identity?
How do they contribute to your journey?

I am unique, and that's what makes me special.

ACCEPTANCE JOURNEY

Write about your journey towards accepting your Therian identity.
What obstacles have you overcome?

What new features or traits would you like to evolve?

CONTINUOUS DEVELOPMENT

How has your Therian identity changed over time?

CONTINUOUS DEVELOPMENT

What inspires you as a Therian?

I'M FREE TO BE ME.

Write about a recent adventure

INSPIRATION

Include quotes, images or anything that sparks your imagination.

KEY WORDS

Animal Self. The animal aspect of a Therian's identity.

Animal Totem. A spiritual symbol or guide, often an animal, that represents a person's inner qualities and strengths. Some Therians use totems to understand their connection to their animal identity.

Awakening. The process or moment when a person realises their Therian identity and begins to understand and explore their connection to their animal.

Dream Shift (D-shift). When a Therian dreams of being their animal identity.

Fursona. A character representing a person's animal identity, more common in the furry community but sometimes used by Therians. It serves as an avatar or representation of oneself, often featuring a unique name, personality and appearance that blends human and animal traits.

Howl. A gathering of Therians, often in nature, where they can share experiences, celebrate their animal connections and engage in activities that express their identities.

Instincts. Natural behaviors or reactions that Therians feel are influenced by their animal identity, such as hunting, fleeing, or social interactions.

Kin. Short for otherkin, a related community where individuals identify as non-human beings which can include mythical creatures like elves or dragons.

Mental Shift (M-shift). A shift in mindset where a Therian thinks or behaves like their animal identity.

Pack. A group of Therians who come together, often forming close-knit communities based on their shared animal identities and experiences.

P-shift (Physical Shift). A hypothetical transformation where a Therian's physical body changes to match their animal form, often considered a fantasy within the Therian community.

Phantom Shift (P-shift). A sensory experience where a Therian feels the presence of animal body parts, such as tails or ears, that aren't physically there.

Quads. This is when someone moves around on their hands and feet, walking like a four-legged animal, such as a wolf or a cat.

Shift. A change in the way a Therian feels or behaves, where they experience themselves more like their animal identity. Types include:

- Mental Shift (M-shift)
- Phantom Shift (P-shift)
- Dream Shift (D-shift)

Therian. A person who identifies as having a deep connection to a particular animal, often feeling that this animal is a part of their inner self.

Therianthropy. The belief or feeling of having a spiritual or psychological connection to an animal, which is considered an integral part of one's identity.

Printed in Dunstable, United Kingdom